I CAN'T
F*cking
ADULT
TODAY

A JOURNAL FOR THE DAYS WHEN
YOU'D RATHER STAY IN BED

Monica Sweeney

Bestselling author of *Zen as F*ck*

Castle Point Books
New York

www.castlepointbooks.com

The Castle Point Books trademark is owned by Castle Point Publishing, LLC.
Castle Point books are published and distributed by St. Martin's Press.

ISBN 978-1-250-27210-2 (trade paperback)

Cover and interior design by Tara Long

Images used under license from Shutterstock.com

Our books may be purchased in bulk for promotional, educational, or
business use. Please contact your local bookseller or the Macmillan
Corporate and Premium Sales Department at 1-800-221-7945, extension 5442,
or by email at MacmillanSpecialMarkets@macmillan.com.

First Edition: April 2020

10 9 8 7 6 5 4 3 2 1

THIS
JOURNAL
BELONGS
TO

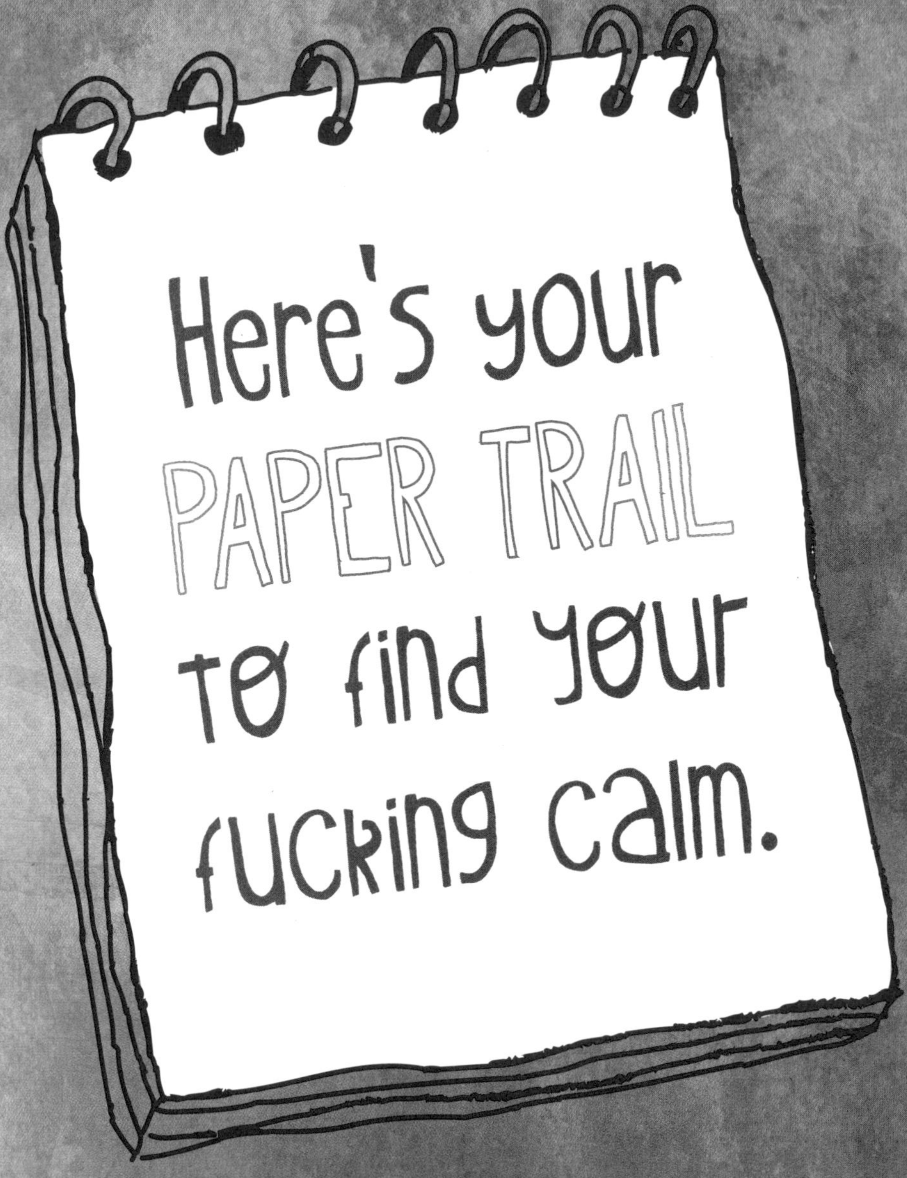
Here's your
PAPER TRAIL
to find your
fucking calm.

The BS-FREE Space

NEED A BREAK FROM ALL THE CRAP weighing you down? Pretending that you know what the fuck you're doing all the time sure is exhausting, so give yourself permission to step away from stressing over finances, responsibilities, and what comes next in the grand plan. Instead of keeping your anxieties bottled up like a fine wine, break those suckers out for a toast.

Go find your space—maybe even a blanket fort! Move aside the piles of papers and to-do lists. Turn off the national news and your social-media notifications. Make cereal for dinner. Drop the filters—and your pants, if you like—and make your alone time just what you need. If you've got complaints, dreams, and a pen, this is the book to confide in. Here, there are no rules other than "You do fucking you."

Start from the beginning with a page a day, or open to a page at random when you need it. Clear away the clusterfuck of adulting with journaling catharsis, spend time just taking a breath, and restore a shit-ton of sanity and energy on the pages of *I Can't Fucking Adult Today*.

Escape THE SHITSHOW

If you could open a trapdoor from your life and enter another realm that is just a little fucking better, where would you be? What makes you want to be there?

What feel-good aspects of this place can you smuggle back into your real life?

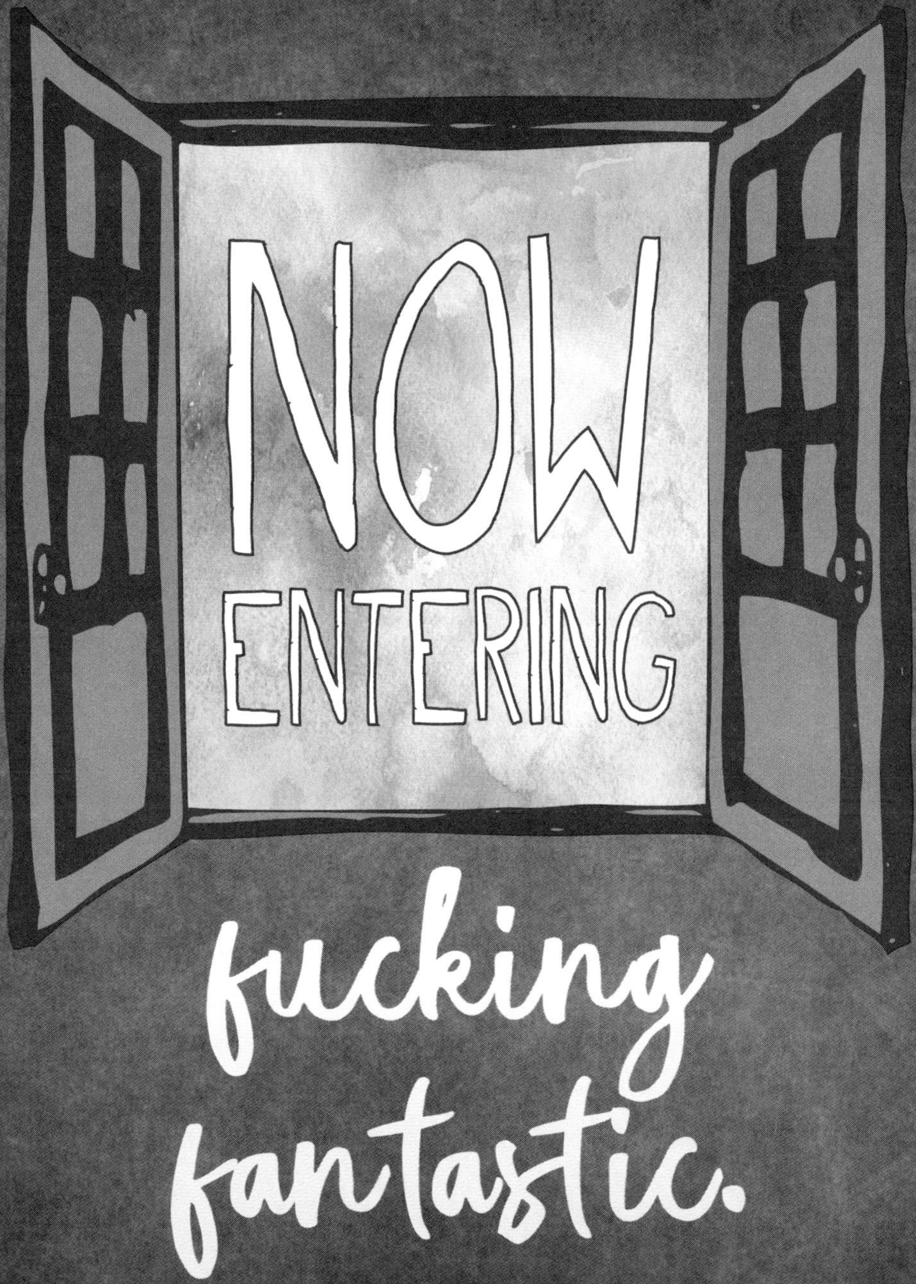
NOW
ENTERING
fucking
fantastic.

STOP Running

Who are you still chasing after that leaves you feeling like crap? A friend who's forgotten you in the shimmer of her own tiara, a crush who ghosted you, a family member who made the choice to walk away a long time ago? Stop tugging on their fucking sleeve. Write the break-up letter for all time here, then carry the fuck on with your best life.

PRESSURE Valve

Sometimes it's okay to just be...okay. When we're always
looking for that blow-your-mind moment, we push aside all the
little (but good!) shit that makes the day pretty bearable. Take
a moment to look up—even one little ray of fucking sunshine
sneaking through the dusty mini blinds of life can help.
What went okay for you today?

FUCK the Haters

Write your name on the label across from this page. Then cover this page with all the bullshit labels you've ever been called to your face, behind your back, or on social media. Maybe there are some shitty labels you give yourself when you're down.

Sure you've got them all? There's space on the back of this page as well. (Yep, go fucking crazy!) Once you're feeling confident you've got them covered, tear out this page and choose your weapon of destruction—maybe the shredder, or just your bare hands! You can't stop the name-calling completely, but you can let that shit go so it doesn't rule your world.

COME ON In

What kick-ass people or places (physical, like a coffee shop, or virtual, like an online community) accept you no matter what your mood is? When have they seen you at your worst and not fucking flinched?

Strong-Ass ANCHORS

When you feel surrounded by douchebags and their tsunamis of crap, what fucking beautiful moments in your day keep you from drowning? They can be super simple. Maybe it's drinking from a favorite mug in the morning or barking back at that crazy dog down the street when you go by every day. Write or draw them here.

I will not
get
lost in

A SHITWAVE
OF DRAMA.

That's my
GIVE-NO-FUCKS
FREQUENCY.

Playlist THERAPY

Music and moods are a hella perfect pairing. Which songs help you

...get out a good ugly cry?

_____

...pick up an otherwise pissy day?

_____

...vent your anger?

_____

...feel like a boss bitch?

_____

...LOL?

_____

It's time to
UNLOCK
YOUR
BADASS.

Let It OUT

What did you want to say to someone so fucking badly today? Maybe you held back because the words would stir up a total clusterfuck you're not ready to handle, or maybe the right words only came to you when the moment was past. Release them here and now.

Cut THAT SHIT OUT

Putting on phony-ass masks for others can be exhausting.
What are you pretending to be that you're not? Why the
act—and is it worth the energy to keep that shit up? If not,
what's your exit scene?

CAPED Confessions

You are strong as fuck when you know your weaknesses. When you can embrace your flaws with a big fucking hug, no one can use them against you. List some of your biggest struggles below. Are you the bitch queen of procrastination, a rebel without a filter, or a fucking tornado of moods? How can you turn these flaws into something to appreciate, or at least joke about with all of the other glorious fuck-ups in your life?

Feelings Forecast

Emotions can be as unpredictable as the weather. How would you describe your state of mind in weather terms right now? Shitballs of record size or sunny with no chance of BS? If you're trending toward shitballs, what's the last thing you remember that made you feel full of fucking sunshine?

MEET
my
treasures.

Top FIVE

While the shit you own isn't everything, certain objects can carry happy-ass vibes. What five things mean the most to you?

1. --

----

2. --

----

3. --

----

4. --

----

5. --

Mine, All Mine!

Feel like there's a constant tug on your time? Imagine you have an entire day to simply live the shit out of life. What's your pleasure?

How can you make even just a motherfucking part (or feeling) of that day come true soon?

Can I get
a damn
DO-OVER?

Real Regrets

What recent fuckups in your life do you most wish you could apply autocorrect to?

Even if you can't take things back completely, is there anything you can do to smooth the situation so you can carry the fuck on?

Hello, ruckwit?!

"I love you." "I hate you." "We need to talk." Who needs a big-ass billboard to get a fucking clue—and what is the message you're sending?

GO There

Think of a time you felt like you were on top of the fucking world. Where were you and what were you doing?

Can you find a way to re-create that feeling when the crap of life hits and you need a boost?

MY SANITY
is protected
property.

Fuck Off!

You now rule your own private island. If any old fucker wants to come and live here, what are the top rules they need to follow?

Do any of these rules inspire boundaries you can set to guard against the bullshit in your real life?

NAME THE Hurricanes

Fucking Category 5 hurricanes are inevitable in nature and in our lives. Who are the hellish hurricanes in your life, and what's their damage level?

What's your recovery plan to emerge unscathed from the rubble when these assholes strike?

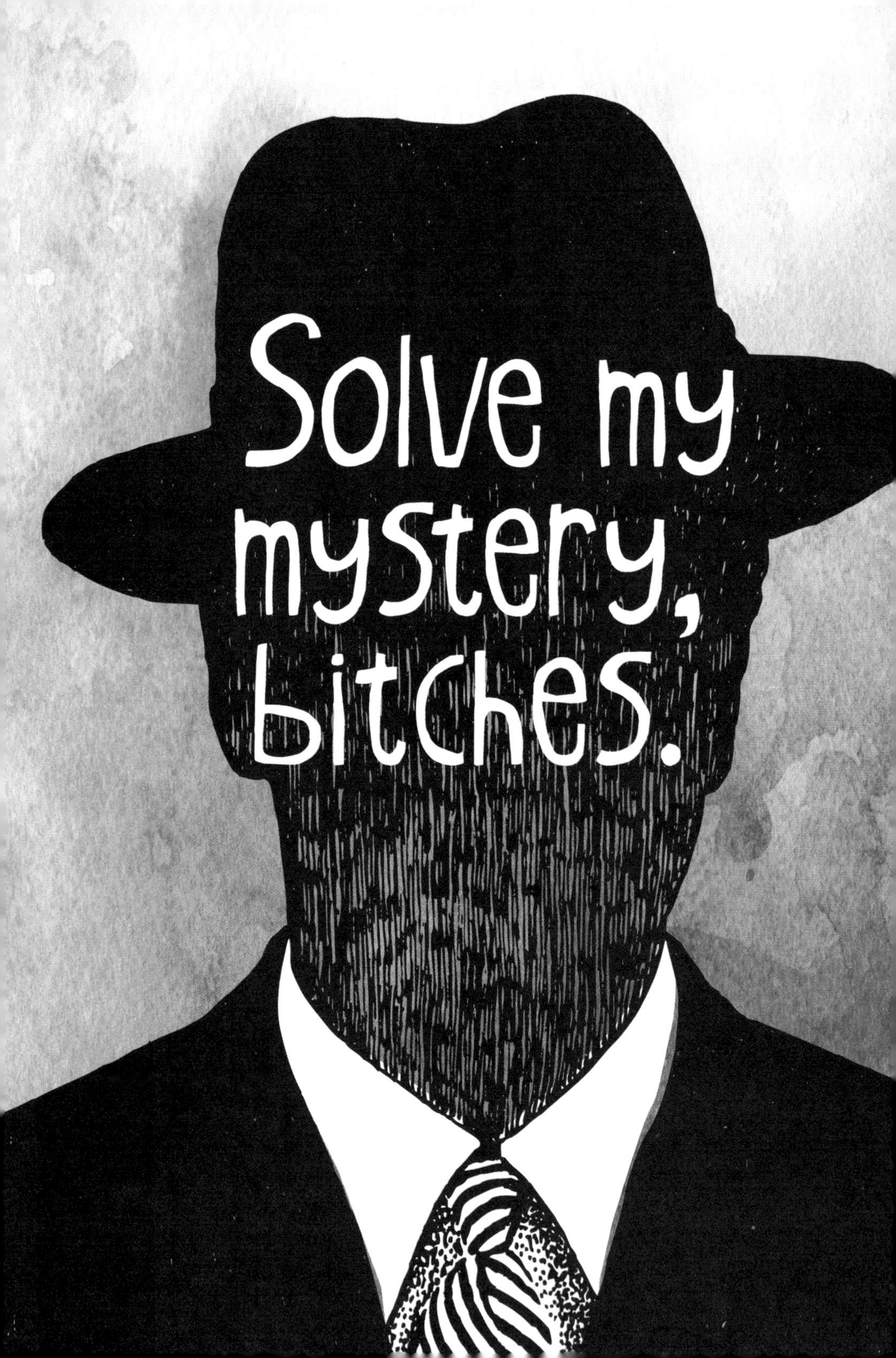
Solve my mystery, bitches.

It's Our Secret

What's one thing no one knows about you? Why haven't you shared it with anyone? Will you ever let it out beyond these pages?

Can I get the
ANSWER KEY?

No Fucking Clue

Big or small, what one question have you always wanted answered? Is there a way to get the answer—or at least edge a little closer?

We're all a little afraid of the dark.

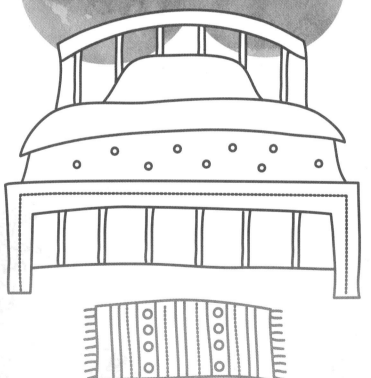

Motherfucking Monsters

There are probably a crapload of nightmares and irrational fears you've outgrown. But what still makes you want to crawl into the fetal position under your covers?

What makes you feel safe?

Be in the moment, not the fucking selfie.

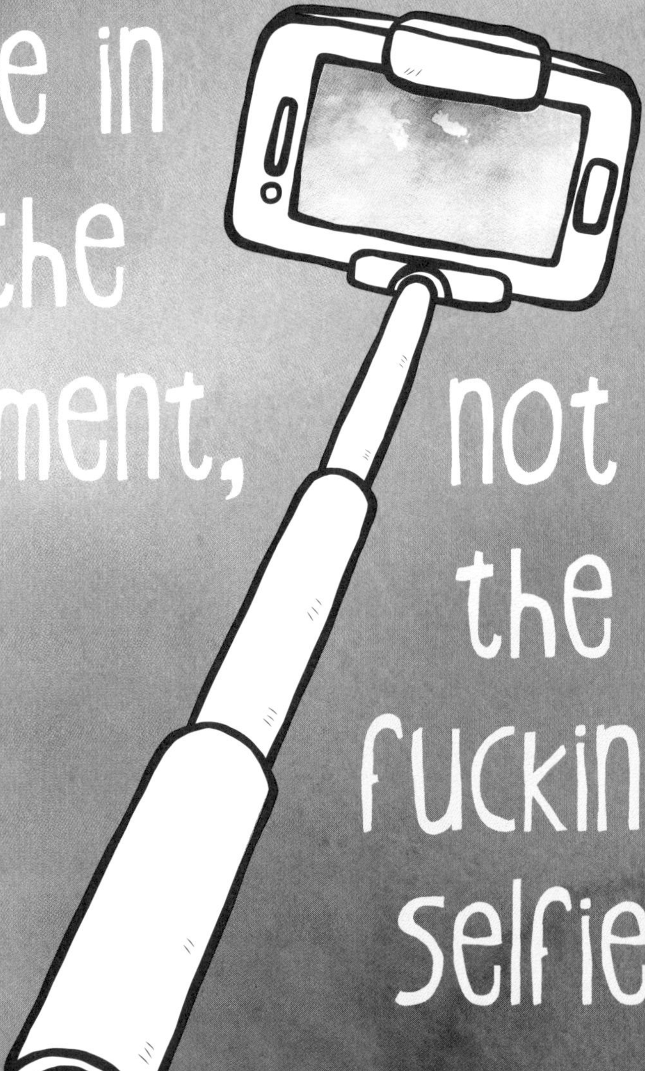

True Portraits

Find a photo in which you're smiling or laughing (not posed, fucking real!). Attach it below and recall what you were doing and anyone who was with you. Make a plan to do that thing or connect with those friends this week.

Rep Reveal

We love to say we don't give a shit what others think. But it's only natural to wonder about others' impressions of you. What do you want people to say about you when you're not around?

Are there healthy changes you can make to boost the fucking positive vibes you give off?

Give me
VITAMIN
D-AAMN
skies.

Outdoor Recess

When you just need to get away, where can you go outdoors
to breathe in fucking freedom and breathe out the bullshit?

Worlds COLLIDE

If your online personality (from social media to dating profiles) came off the screen into real fucking life, in what ways would you be clones? In what ways would you not even recognize each other?

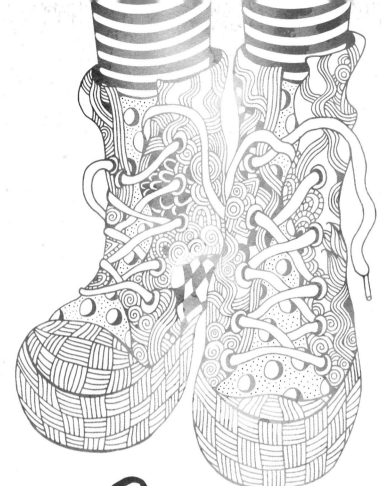

Stay
weird.

Celebrate the Crazy

Isn't a little fucking ridiculous better than totally fucking boring?
List 10 things about yourself that are weird as fuck but wonderful.

1. ....

2. ....

3. ....

4. ....

5. ....

6. ....

7. ....

8. ....

9. ....

10. ....

Come with me into the fucking deep.

Out of the Shallow

Sometimes we keep our depths hidden, afraid to reveal the good and bad shit that sits at our core. What do people not see when they first meet you that you wish they would discover sooner?

All Kinds of GOALS

Why so serious? Not all goals need to center on career, finances, and all that heavy shit. What goals will make you say "Fuck, yeah!" in your real life in the next year?

WATCH MORE
sunsets
THAN
Netflix.

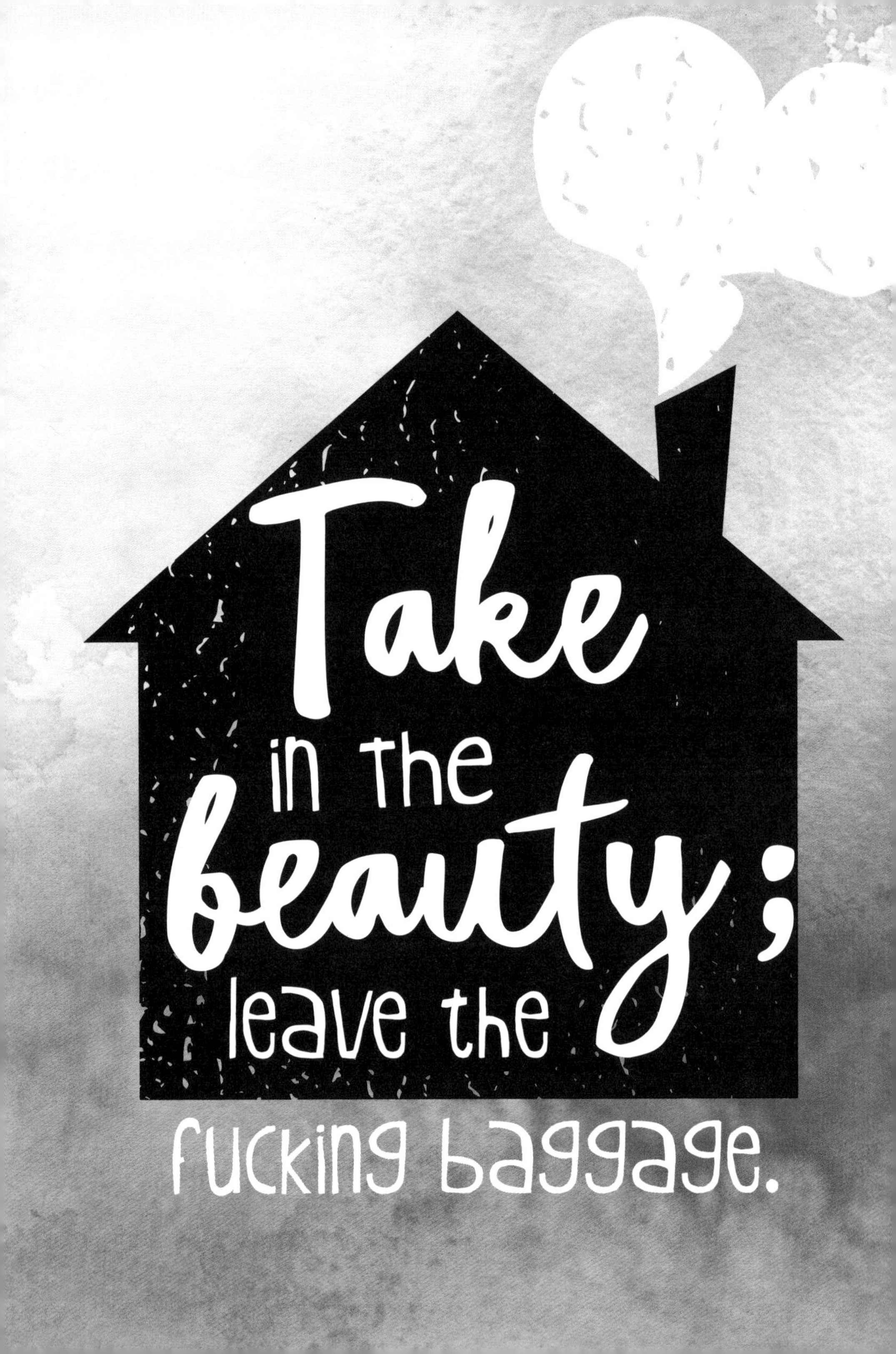
Take
in the
beauty;
leave the
fucking baggage.

Hell or a Place to Live

Cities and towns come with their own peculiar flavor. How does where you live make your life fucking amazing? What can you discover and do right where you are?

_____

_____

_____

_____

_____

How does where you live make days challenging? What limitations do you want to tell to fuck off, and how can you get past them?

_____

_____

_____

_____

_____

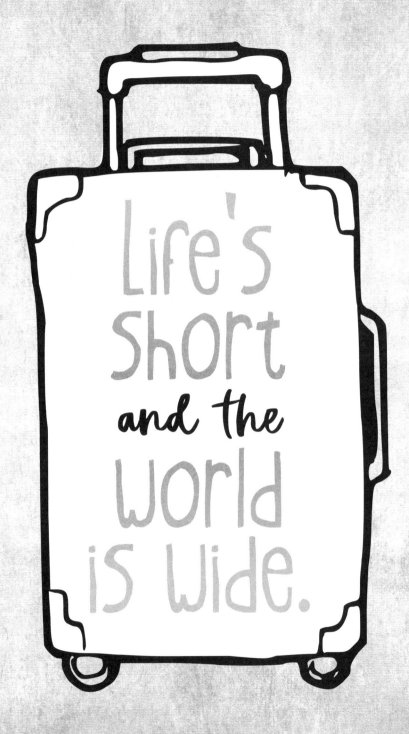

Badass Adventurer

What destinations do you dream of traveling to?

What do you need to do to just fucking go?

Shit That Speaks to Me

Whether they come from an author, a celebrity, your best friend, or a family member, what words of wisdom, inspiration, or venting hold special meaning for you? At what moments in your life have they helped you?

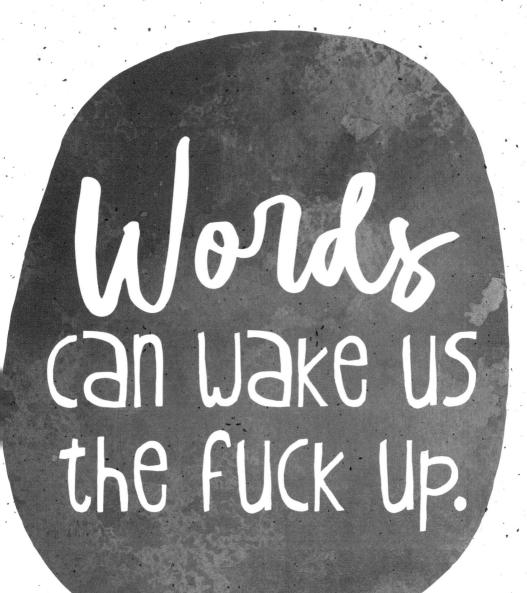

Love your decisions,
not others' opinions of them.

Sounds About Right

We make tons of choices every day—and some turn out better than others, to say the least. What's the best fucking choice you've ever made?

How did you know it was the right choice at the time?

Release That Crap

Holding in emotions and keeping it all fucking together 24/7 can be a setup for a major crash. It's healthy to allow some release before it comes to a full-on break. When was the last time you cried?

_____

_____

_____

_____

_____

How did you feel afterward?

_____

_____

_____

_____

_____

BE
BETTER
than BASIC.

Do Hard Things

There are always going to be two paths in life: the nice, easy one and the fucking off-road adventure full of potholes and detours. And they usually lead to very different places and degrees of rewards. What hard thing have you done that you once thought you never could do and how did it feel to take that path?

What's the next challenge you need to conquer?

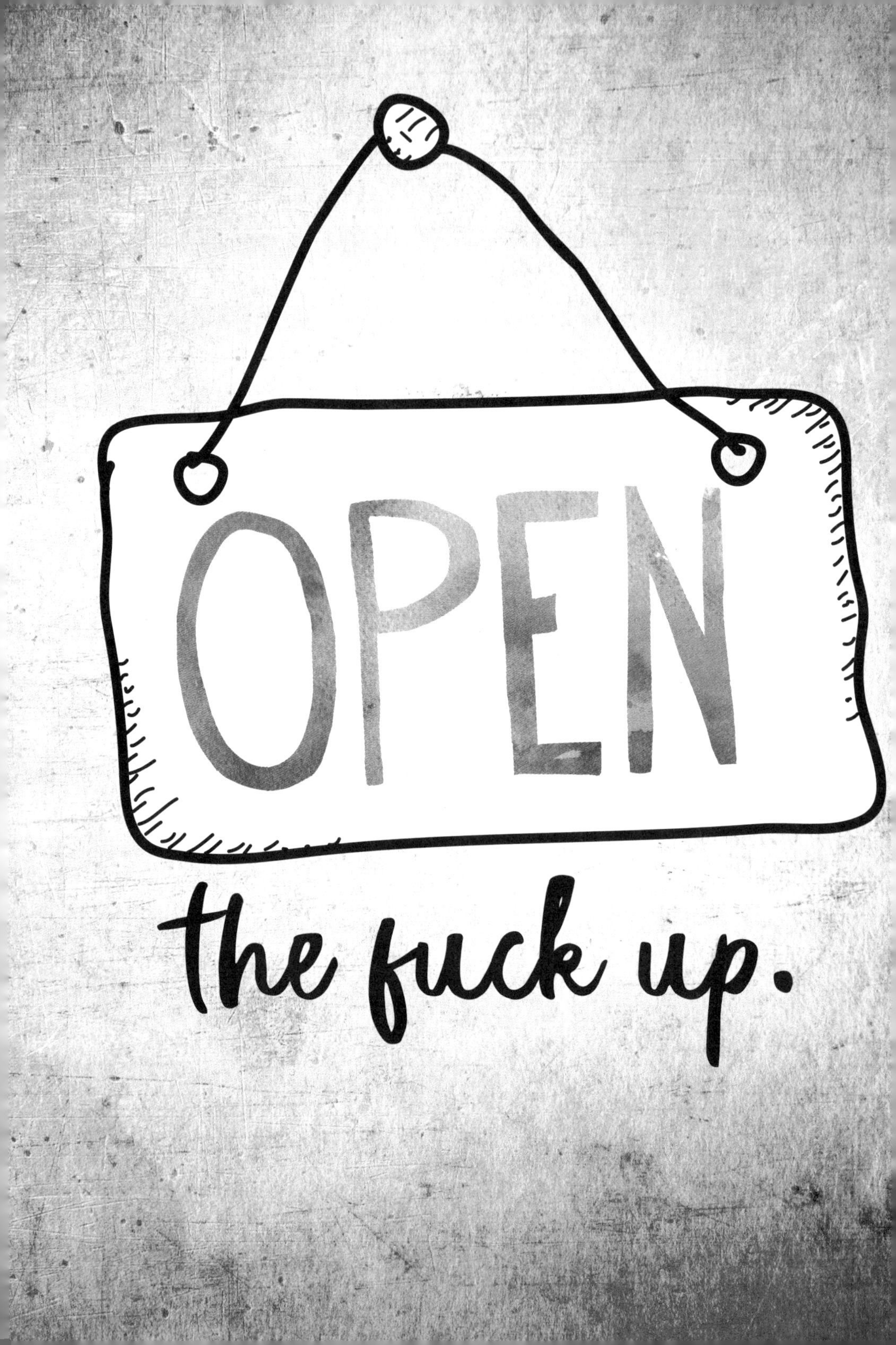
OPEN
the fuck up.

Sorry for the Slam!

There's a saying that goes, "Happiness often sneaks in a door
you didn't think was open." Are there people or experiences
in your life that you slammed the door on too fucking
quickly? How can you let them know that the door is inching
open again?

STORY Support

When you write the fucking magnificent story of your life,
whose name(s) do you want to appear in it a billion times?
What has earned them that position?

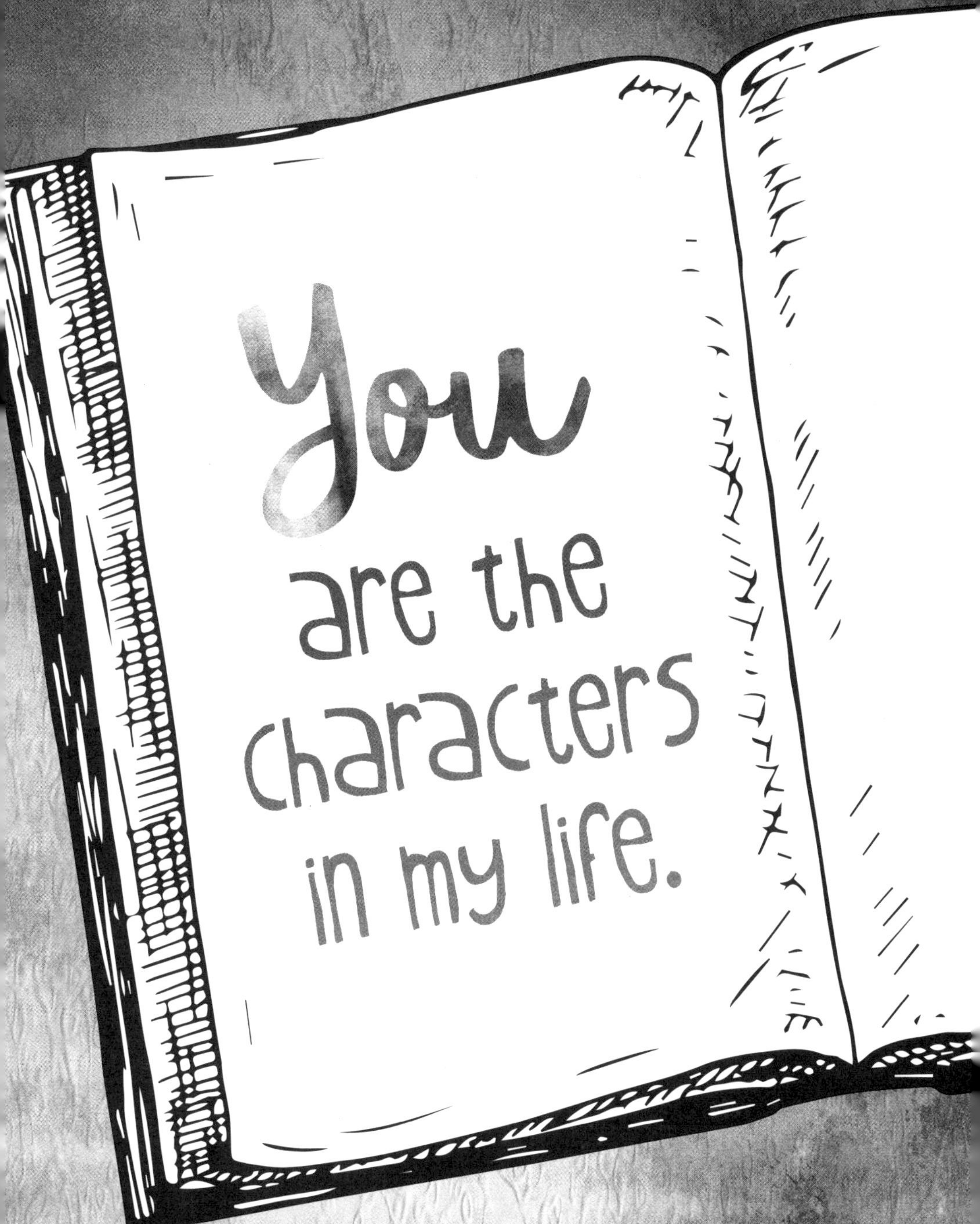
You
are the
characters
in my life.

Me vs. the World

What do you see very differently than everyone around you?
Does it bother you that no one else fucking relates?

Why do you think you have a different idea?

Smiles and Smiles

Cover this page with the random (big and little!) shit that makes you happy.

Face It

What have you been putting off—a decision, a conversation, an apology? Decide now when and where you will stop the flight and move the fuck forward.

I'll PASS, Dumbass

What has everyone been making a huge-ass deal over lately that clearly doesn't deserve your time and attention?

How can you walk away, down whatever fucking road, without adding to the drama?

Kick-Ass Expectations

What fan-fucking-tastic things are you looking forward to in the next few months?

In the next few years?

Yas Queen

Who can you count on to always put a big-ass smile on your face? Remember five times this person came to your rescue and pulled you out of crappy situations or moods.

1. ....

....

2. ....

....

3. ....

....

4. ....

....

5. ....

....

Before and After

Maybe it was meeting someone new. It could have been a text or call that cleared up a misunderstanding. Or did you finally reach a goal you set for yourself? What fucking spectacular moments from the past year changed everything for you?

TIME TO *Reverse*

Is there shit you've gotten pulled into that isn't yours to own?
How can you back out and let the true parties involved take it
from here?

Leave Shit Undone

Some retreat from the craziness is okay. What's your favorite way to be lazy as hell, and how do you limit the kick-back time so it doesn't kick your ass in your relationships and adult roles?

enter at your own fucking risk.

ng risk. enter at your own fuckin

Construction Zone

What part of your life feels like it's constantly under a crap ton of construction—maybe even demolition?

What acts as your safety helmet as you go through the shit zone?

NEVER FUCK
with the
QUEEN.

All Hail?

Would your friends characterize you as queen of hearts or hell queen, and why? Is the answer the same for your family?

_____

_____

_____

_____

_____

_____

Are you okay with this assessment or would you like to show them another side they're not seeing?

_____

_____

_____

_____

_____

No More Delays

What have you always wanted to do that you keep putting off? How can you get out of your own fucking way and make that adventure or wish come to life this year?

Surprise, Ass-hats!

Who is underestimating you in your life right now?
How will you prove those motherfuckers wrong?

I Fucking LOVE YOU

We often get into the biggest emotional conflicts with the people we care about most. If we didn't give a shit, we wouldn't put up a fuss. What's the worst fight you've ever had?

....

....

....

....

....

How did the relationship get repaired, or are you still working on it?

....

....

....

....

....

You're
worth
all the gold
in the world.

Until I saw this,

I didn't
know what
fucking
beautiful meant.

Through My Eyes

What do you consider beautiful? Use words, photos, and drawings to capture beauty below.

Not luck.

I full-fuck deserved it.

The Payoff

What is something you worked really fucking hard for and poured your soul into, and it paid off? How did the effort feel? How did the result feel?

Head vs. Heart

Which do you tend to follow? Do the results turn out
to be fucking gold or absolute crap?

Is there a way to find a balance between your head
and your heart?

HEAD UP,

HEART
STRONG AF.

What's trending?

Being fucking real.

Your Own Course

Hashtag today, headass tomorrow. What trend are you proud of yourself for not following?

Is there a positive trend you've started or could start to show the fuckers what really matters?

We're all JUST KIDS who left the playground.

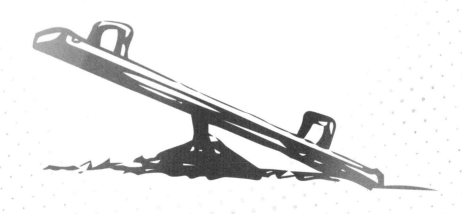

Growing the Fuck Up

What did you think it would be like to be an adult when you were younger? What parts turned out to be true to a fucking fault and where were you way off in your expectations?

No Returns Allowed

We often spend too much time imagining the shitty parts of ourselves we'd love to change. What fucking amazing parts of yourself would you never want to trade in?

NEVER STOP
making memories.

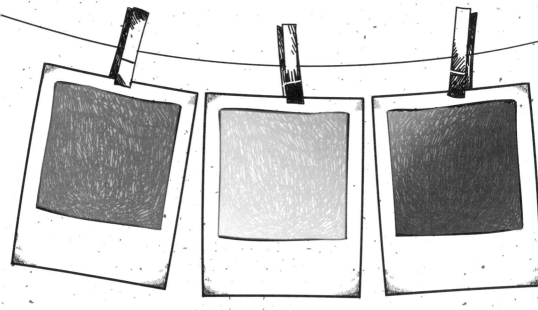

Back Again, BITCH?

If you could return to any day of your life so far and relive it just one more time from start to fucking finish, which day would you choose, and why?

These ass-hats
aren't perfect,

but they're
mine.

Fam Life

If you could change three things about your crazy-ass family, what would they be?

1. _____

_____

2. _____

_____

3. _____

_____

What fucking beautiful sides of your family would you never want to change?

_____

_____

_____

_____

If you're
going to fail,

make it epic.

NO Flying Fucks

Some wiseass in your life has probably told you, "You can't have everything." They're probably right! What are three things you're terrible at—but you totally don't give a fuck?

1. ....

....

....

2. ....

....

....

3. ....

....

....

Ten Reasons Why

What words would your friends use to describe you and why they give a million fucks about your relationship and spending time with you?

1. --

2. --

3. --

4. --

5. --

6. --

7. --

8. --

9. --

10. ---

REAL
AF FRIENDSHIP
is everything.

Exit PLAN

What isn't worth an ounce of your fucking mental energy right now? Consider your activities, relationships, doubts, and fears. Write below what you need to release, then rip out the page and send it flying as a paper airplane or crumple it into a ball targeted for the trash—whichever style is right for you. Then see yourself really fucking soar.